Samsur Ultra U Seniors and Beginners

Simple Step-by-Step Manual to Setup, Configure and Master Your Phone, Camera, and AI Features

Wise Sam

Table of Contents

Chapter 1: Getting Started with Your New Samsung Galaxy S26 Ultra................................ 6

    1.1 Getting to Know Your Device's Physical Features (The Buttons and Ports)................ 11

    1.2 Inserting the SIM and Memory Card..... 15

    1.3 Powering On and The Initial Setup........ 16

Chapter 2: Understanding the Hardware & Basics.. 24

    2.1 Front, Side, and Top Views (A Closer Look) 24

    2.2 Your Magical S Pen: An Introduction..... 28

    2.3 Charging the Battery and Power Saving 30

Chapter 3: Device Setup & Accounts.............. 35

    3.1 Connecting to Wi-Fi and Mobile Networks 35

    3.2 Your Google and Samsung Accounts..... 38

    3.3 Setting Up Security: Locking Your Digital Door 40

Chapter 4: Core Functions & Communication 46

4.1 Making and Receiving Phone Calls 46

4.2 Managing Your Contacts (Your Digital Address Book) 50

4.3 Sending Messages (SMS & MMS) 52

4.4 Using Email 54

4.5 Browsing the Internet with Samsung Internet 56

Chapter 5: Galaxy AI Features 60

5.1 Introduction to Galaxy AI 60

5.2 Circle to Search & Google Gemini Integration 62

5.3 Live Translate & Interpreter 64

5.4 AI Camera & Editing Tools (Your Digital Photo Lab) 66

5.5 Now Brief & Seamless Actions 70

Chapter 6: Camera Guide 74

6.1 Camera Overview & Interface 74

6.2 Core Photo & Video Modes 78

6.3 Advanced Features 81

6.4 Tips for Taking Great Photos 83

Chapter 7: Customization & Settings 87

7.1 Home Screen, Apps Screen, and Widgets
.... 87

7.2 Themes, Wallpapers, and Always On Display (AOD) 91

7.3 Sound and Vibration Settings 93

7.4 Notifications and the Quick Panel 96

Chapter 8: Productivity & Advanced Features
.... 100

8.1 Samsung DeX: Your Phone as a PC 100

8.2 Multi-Window & Split-Screen for Multitasking 102

8.3 Samsung Pass for Secure Logins 103

8.4 Samsung Health & SmartThings Integration 104

Introduction

Congratulations on your new Samsung Galaxy S26 Ultra! You're holding a device with an incredible amount of power and potential, capable of connecting you with family, capturing precious memories, and opening up a world of information and entertainment.

But let's be honest, all those dazzling features can feel a little overwhelming. Where do you even begin? If you've ever felt frustrated by technology that seems designed for someone half your age, you're not alone. Many user manuals are written by engineers, for engineers, filled with technical jargon that leaves you more confused than when you started.

This book is different.

This guide was written with one simple goal: to give you **confidence and control** over your new phone. We've stripped away the confusing technical language and replaced it with clear, patient, and easy-to-follow instructions.

In this book, you will discover how to:

- **Set Up with Ease:** We'll walk you through the initial setup. From inserting your SIM card to connecting to Wi-Fi, with large, clear texts to guide you every step of the way.

- **Master the Essentials:** Learn the core skills effortlessly: making and receiving calls, sending text messages and emails, taking stunning photos, and adjusting settings like volume and brightness to suit your needs.

- **Unlock "Hidden" Features:** This is where the real fun begins! We'll show you clever tricks the phone doesn't always tell you about, like using your voice to command the phone, simplifying the home screen, and using the advanced camera features to take perfect pictures of your grandchildren.

- **Stay Safe and Secure:** Learn simple steps to protect your privacy, avoid common online scams, and keep your personal information safe.

We've designed every chapter to be a stress-free experience. Each step is broken down into bite-sized pieces, and tips pointing out what each icon and button does. You can read this book from cover to cover, or simply jump to the chapter that solves the problem you have right now.

Your Samsung Galaxy S26 Ultra is a powerful tool designed to make your life richer and more connected, not more complicated. It's time to stop feeling intimidated and start feeling empowered.

Let's begin your journey to total mastery!

A Quick Note Before You Start:

This guide is an **unofficial, independent resource** created to help you get the most from your device. It is not endorsed by or affiliated with Samsung Electronics Co., Ltd. All trademarks, including Samsung and

Galaxy, are the property of their respective owners.

Chapter 1: Getting Started with Your New Samsung Galaxy S26 Ultra

Welcome to your new phone! This chapter will guide you through the very first steps, from holding the phone for the first time to getting it ready for use. We'll go slowly and explain everything in simple terms.

1.1 Getting to Know Your Device's Physical Features (The Buttons and Ports)

Before we turn it on, let's learn the parts of the phone. This will make the next steps much easier.

- **The Front:**
    - **Large Screen:** This is a touchscreen. You will tap, swipe, and type on this surface.

- **Front Camera:** A small, pinhole-like lens at the top of the screen for taking selfies and video calls.
- **Earpiece:** A thin slit at the top edge where you will hear the sound during a phone call.

- **The Sides (Right and Left):**
  - **Right Side:**
    - **Power / Side Key:** This is the most important button. It turns your phone on and off. You will also use it to lock the screen when you're not using the phone.
    - **Volume Keys:** Two buttons right above the Power key. The top one

makes sounds louder, and the bottom one makes them quieter or puts the phone on silent.

- Left Side:

  - **S Pen Slot:** This is where the special S Pen stylus is stored. To remove it, just press it in gently until you feel a click, and then pull it out. To put it back, just push it in until it clicks again.

  - **SIM / Memory Card Tray:** A small, thin tray that holds your phone's SIM card (which connects you to your mobile network).

- **The Bottom Edge:**

    o **USB-C Port:** This is where you plug in the charging cable. The cable will only fit one way, so don't force it.

    o **Main Speaker:** A series of small holes where most of the sound (music, videos, ringtones) comes from.

    o **Microphone:** A tiny hole for picking up your voice.

- **The Top Edge:**

    o **Another Microphone:** Used for noise cancellation during calls.

1.2 Inserting the SIM and Memory Card

Important: Your phone needs a SIM card from your mobile provider (like AT&T, Verizon, T-Mobile) to make calls and use mobile data.

- **What You'll Need:** The SIM ejector tool (a small metal pin that came in the box with your phone).

- **Step 1:** Find the small pinhole on the left side of the phone, next to the S Pen slot.

- **Step 2:** Gently push the SIM ejector tool into the pinhole. The tray will pop out slightly.

- **Step 3:** Carefully pull the tray all the way out.

- **Step 4:** Place your SIM card into the tray. It will only fit one way, so match the notched corner of the card to the notch in the tray.

- **Step 5:** Gently slide the tray back into the phone until it clicks and is flush with the side.

1.3 Powering On and The Initial Setup

This is the first time you'll turn on your phone. It will guide you through a series of simple steps to get it ready.

- **Step 1: Turn it On**

    - Press and hold the **Power / Side Key** on the right side for a few seconds. You will feel a small vibration and see the Samsung logo on the screen.

- **Step 2: Select Your Language**
    - The screen will ask you to choose a language. Tap on your preferred language (e.g., "English").
- **Step 3: Connect to a Wi-Fi Network**
    - Your phone will show a list of available Wi-Fi networks. Wi-Fi is a wireless internet connection, like the one you might have at home.
    - Tap on the name of your home Wi-Fi network.
    - A keyboard will appear on the screen. Type in your Wi-Fi password carefully (it's usually on a sticker on your router).

- o   Tap "Connect." **Tip:** Connecting to Wi-Fi for setup saves your mobile data and makes the process faster.
- **Step 4: Copy Apps & Data (This is a very helpful step!)**
  - o   If you are switching from an old Android phone or an iPhone, this phone can help you transfer your contacts, photos, and more.
  - o   The phone will ask if you want to "Copy apps and data." Tap "Next."
  - o   You will be given a choice:
    - **From an Android phone?** Use the "Smart Switch" app.

- **From an iPhone?** Follow the on-screen instructions to connect the two phones.
    - You can also choose "Don't copy" if you are setting up a brand-new phone.
- **Step 5: Sign In to Your Google Account**
    - Your phone uses a Google account (this is the same as a Gmail account). If you have one, enter your email and password. If you don't have one, you can create a new one here.
    - **Why is this important?** This account backs up your photos, saves your contacts, and lets you

download apps from the Play Store.

- **Step 6: Set Up Security (Protecting Your Phone)**

    o The phone will ask how you want to unlock it. This is very important for privacy and security.

    o **Recommended for Seniors:** Set up a **PIN** (a 4-6 digit number you'll remember) or a **Pattern** (a simple swipe pattern on the screen). These are easy to use and very secure.

    o You can also set up more advanced options like

Fingerprint or Face Recognition later.

- **Step 7: Set Up Samsung Account & Google Services**
    - You may be prompted to sign in or create a free Samsung account. This gives you access to special Samsung features and backup.
    - You will also see a few screens about Google services. It's safe and recommended to leave the default options selected and tap "Accept" or "Next."
- **Step 8: You're All Set!**
    - After a final loading screen, you will see your new home screen.

Congratulations, your phone is now ready to use!

Key Tips for Beginners & Seniors:

- **Don't Worry About Mistakes:** You can't break the phone by tapping the wrong thing. If you get lost, pressing the **Power Key** once to turn off the screen, and then pressing it again to wake it up, is a good way to start over.

- **The "Back" Gesture:** To go back to the previous screen, simply swipe your finger from the left or right edge of the screen towards the center. This is the most common navigation gesture.

- **Ask for Help:** If a step is confusing, don't hesitate to ask a family member or friend to help you. The initial setup is the hardest part, and it gets much easier from here

Chapter 2: Understanding the Hardware & Basics

Now that your phone is set up, this chapter will help you get familiar with the physical parts of your device and its everyday functions. Think of this as learning where the lights and wipers are in a new car.

2.1 Front, Side, and Top Views (A Closer Look)

Let's review the physical features in more detail, now that the screen is on.

- **The Front View (When the Screen is On):**

    - **Status Bar:** Look at the very top of the screen. You'll see small icons. This is your status bar. It shows you important information at a glance:

- **Cell Signal Bars**
  (📶): How strong your mobile network connection is.

- **Wi-Fi Symbol**
  (📶): Appears when you're connected to Wi-Fi.

- **Battery Percentage**
  (🔋 84%):** Shows how much battery life is left.

- **Time:** The current time.

○ **Navigation Bar (Gesture Controls):** Your phone uses "gestures" instead of buttons at the bottom of the screen. It's simple!

- **Go Home:** Swipe up from the very bottom of the screen. This will always take you back to your main home screen.

- **Go Back:** Swipe from the left or right edge of the screen towards the center. This is like a "back" button and is one of the most useful gestures.

- **See Recent Apps:** Swipe up from the bottom and hold your finger for a second. You'll see all your open apps like a deck of cards, and you can swipe to close them or tap to switch to one.

- **The Sides and Top (In Daily Use):**

    - **Power / Side Key:** A short press **locks** the screen, putting the phone to sleep. A long press (hold for 2 seconds) wakes up **Bixby** (Samsung's voice assistant) or, if you hold it longer, gives you the option to power off.

    - **Pro Tip:** You can double-press the Power Key to quickly open the camera—great for capturing a fast-moving moment!

    - **Volume Keys:** Use these to adjust ringtone, media, and alarm volume. When the screen is off, pressing them will still adjust your ringer volume.

2.2 Your Magical S Pen: An Introduction

The S Pen is like a fancy digital pen that comes with your phone. It's stored safely inside the phone itself. Don't be afraid to use it—it's precise and fun!

- **Taking Out the S Pen:** Gently press the end of the S Pen on the bottom-left side. It will pop out slightly. Pull it out completely.

- **What Happens When You Remove It:** A menu of options will appear on the screen. This is called the "Air Command" menu.

- **Simple Things to Try First:**

    1. **Write a Note:** Take out the S Pen while the screen is off and just start writing on the black screen. It will create a quick note you can save.

    2. **Use it as a Pointer:** Use the tip of the S Pen to tap on icons and buttons on the screen instead of your finger. It can be easier to see and more accurate.

    3. **Take a Photo:** Open the Camera app. You can use the button on the side of the S Pen to take a picture from a distance. It's like a camera remote!

- **Putting It Back:** Just push the S Pen back into its slot until it clicks. The phone will tell you if it's securely stored.

2.3 Charging the Battery and Power Saving

Keeping your phone charged is easy. You don't need to let it drain completely; modern phone batteries are happy with partial charges.

- **How to Charge (Wired):**

    1. Take the USB-C cable that came with your phone.

    2. Plug the smaller, oval-shaped end into the **USB-C port** at the bottom of your phone. It only fits one way.

3. Plug the other end into the power adapter (the "block") and then into a wall outlet.

- **How to Charge (Wireless - Optional):**

    1. If you buy a wireless charger, you simply place the middle of your phone's back flat on the charging pad. A light or sound will usually confirm it's charging. No cables needed!

- **Understanding Battery Icons:**

    1. **Charging (⚡):** You'll see a lightning bolt on the battery icon when it's charging.

    2. **Fully Charged (🔋 100%):****The battery icon will be full, and

often the phone will say "Fully charged."

- **Making Your Battery Last Longer:**

    1. **Turn on Power Saving Mode:** If you're going to be away from a charger for a long time, you can go to **Settings > Battery and Device Care > Battery > Power Saving Mode**. This slightly reduces performance to extend battery life.

    2. **Reduce Screen Brightness:** Swipe down from the top of the screen twice to see the Quick Settings panel. Drag the brightness slider a bit to the left.

Key Tips for Beginners & Seniors for Chapter 2:

- **Practice the Gestures:** The "swipe up to go home" and "swipe from the edge to go back" gestures might feel strange at first, but practice for a few minutes. They quickly become second nature and make using the large screen easier.

- **The S Pen is Your Friend:** If you find your finger taps are not as precise as you'd like, try using the S Pen for tasks like typing on the keyboard, clicking small links on a website, or editing photos. It gives you more control.

- **Don't Worry About Wireless Charging:** The cable works perfectly fine. Wireless charging is just a convenient extra if you want to buy the pad later.

- **Your Phone Learns Your Habits:** The battery life might seem short at first, but over a week, the phone will learn how you use it and optimize battery usage to last longer.

Chapter 3: Device Setup & Accounts

This chapter helps you connect your phone to the world and lock the digital door to keep your information safe. We'll cover Wi-Fi, your essential accounts, and security settings.

3.1 Connecting to Wi-Fi and Mobile Networks

Your phone uses two main ways to connect to the internet: Wi-Fi (like your home network) and the Mobile Network (from your carrier, like Verizon or AT&T).

- **Connecting to a Wi-Fi Network (For Home, Cafe, etc.):**

    1. Find and open the **Settings** app on your home screen (it looks like a gear ⚙).

2. Tap on **Connections**.

3. Tap **Wi-Fi**. A switch at the top will turn on. Your phone will automatically search for networks.

4. A list of available networks will appear. Tap the name of **your home Wi-Fi**.

5. A keyboard will pop up. **Carefully type your Wi-Fi password**. If you don't know it, it's often on a sticker on your internet router.

6. Tap **Connect**. The word "Connected" will appear under your network name once you're successful.

- **Why use Wi-Fi?** It's usually faster and doesn't use up the data from your mobile plan. It's best for home, watching videos, and downloading apps.

- **Understanding the Mobile Network (Cellular Data):**

    1. This is the internet connection provided by your phone company. You don't need to set it up—it should just work if you have an active SIM card.

    2. You can turn it off to save data. In **Settings** > **Connections** > **Mobile Networks**, you can toggle "Mobile Data" on or off.

3. **Icon Key:** Look at the top of your screen. You'll see either "**5G**," "**4G**," **or** "**LTE**" when you're connected to the mobile network. You'll see the **Wi-Fi symbol** (📶) when you're connected to Wi-Fi.

3.2 Your Google and Samsung Accounts

Think of these accounts as your phone's "brain" and "memory." They are free and essential.

- **Your Google Account (This is your Gmail account):**
    - **What it does:** This account saves your contacts, backs up your photos to Google Photos, syncs your calendar, and lets you

download apps from the **Play Store**.

- ○ **How to check if you're signed in:** Go to **Settings** > **Accounts and Backup** > **Manage Accounts**. You should see your Google account listed.

- ○ **If you forget your password:** Don't worry! You can reset it on any computer by going to the Gmail website and clicking "Forgot password?"

- **Your Samsung Account:**

  - ○ **What it does:** This unlocks special Samsung features, like using "Find My Mobile" to locate your phone if it's lost, backing up your settings, and accessing Samsung's app store, the **Galaxy Store**.

- ○ **You probably made one during setup.** You can check in **Settings > Accounts and Backup > Manage Accounts**.

- **Key Tip:** It's okay if you mix these up. Just remember you need your Google account for Gmail, Photos, and the Play Store.

3.3 Setting Up Security: Locking Your Digital Door

This is a very important step to protect your personal information and photos if your phone is ever lost or stolen.

- **Where to go:** Open **Settings > Security and Privacy > Device Lock**.

- **Choosing Your Lock Method (We'll start with the simplest):**

    1. **Pattern:**
        - You draw a simple pattern connecting at least four dots.
        - **Good for:** People who find it easier to remember a shape than a number.
        - **Pro Tip:** Make it a little more complex than a simple square or "L" shape.

    2. **PIN (Personal Identification Number):**

- You set a 4- to 6-digit number.

- **Good for:** Most users, especially seniors. It's familiar, like an ATM PIN, and very secure.

- **Pro Tip:** Don't use easy sequences like "1234" or your birth year.

3. **Password:**

    - A longer password with letters, numbers, and symbols.

    - **Good for:** Maximum security, but can be slower to type.

- **Setting Up Fingerprint or Face Recognition (Biometrics):**

    1. These are very convenient and secure. You can set them up *after* you have a Pattern, PIN, or Password. The phone will guide you through the process.

    2. **Fingerprint Unlock:** You'll be asked to place your finger on the screen (the screen itself is the scanner) in different positions until it's fully registered.

    3. **Face Recognition:** The front camera will scan your face. It works best in good lighting.

    4. **Important:** Your Pattern/PIN/Password is

your **backup**. If the fingerprint scanner doesn't work or it's too dark for face recognition, you can always use your PIN to get in.

Key Tips for Beginners & Seniors for Chapter 3:

- **Wi-Fi is Your Friend:** Always connect to Wi-Fi at home. It saves your mobile data for when you're out and about.

- **Write Down Your Password:** It's perfectly safe to write your Wi-Fi password and your phone's unlock PIN in a small, private notebook. This can be a lifesaver if you forget.

- **Start Simple with Security:** If you're new to this, start with a **PIN**. It's the easiest to remember and type. You can always add a fingerprint or face scan later in the Settings.

- **"Find My Mobile" is a Lifesaver:** Make sure your Samsung account is set up. If you lose your phone, you can use a computer to go to the Samsung website, log in, and make your phone ring loudly—even if it's on silent—or see its location on a map.

Chapter 4: Core Functions & Communication

This chapter covers the heart of your phone: making calls, sending messages, and managing your contacts. These are the features that turn your device from a small computer into a powerful communication tool.

4.1 Making and Receiving Phone Calls

The Phone app is one of the most important apps on your device.

- **How to Make a Call:**

    1. Find and tap the green **Phone** icon on your home screen. It usually looks like an old-fashioned telephone handset.

2. You will see a number keypad. Tap the numbers you want to call, just like a traditional phone.

3. Tap the green **Call** button to dial.

- **Other Ways to Make a Call:**

    1. **From your Contacts:** In the Phone app, tap the "Contacts" tab at the bottom. Tap any name in your list to call them.

    2. **Using Voice Assistant:** Press and hold the **Power / Side Key** to activate Bixby and say "Call [Contact's Name]." This is very useful when you're driving or your hands are full.

- **Receiving a Call:**

    1. When someone calls you, the screen will light up with the caller's name (if they are in your contacts).

    2. **To answer:** Swipe the green phone icon **towards the center** of the screen.

    3. **To decline:** Swipe the red phone icon **towards the center** of the screen. This sends the caller directly to your voicemail.

    4. **Pro Tip:** If you're busy, you can tap "**Message**" to send a quick pre-written text like "I'll call you later" without answering.

- **During a Call:**

    1. The screen will show several options.

    2. **Mute** (🙊): Turns off your microphone so the other person can't hear you, but you can still hear them.

    3. **Keypad** (#): Brings up the keypad, useful for navigating automated menus.

    4. **Speaker** (📢): Turns on the loudspeaker so you don't have to hold the phone to your ear.

    5. **Add Call:** Lets you call a second person and merge the calls into a conference.

6. **End Call** (📞): The red button to hang up.

4.2 Managing Your Contacts (Your Digital Address Book)

The Contacts app saves all the phone numbers and email addresses for the people you know.

- **Adding a New Contact:**

    1. Open the **Contacts** app (it looks like a person's silhouette).

    2. Tap the "+" (plus) sign, usually at the bottom of the screen.

    3. Fill in the information: **First Name**, **Last Name**, **Phone**, and **Email**.

    4. Tap **Save** in the top corner.

- **Where Are Contacts Saved?**

    1. It's best to save contacts to your **Google Account**. This way, if you ever lose your phone or get a new one, all your contacts are safely backed up online and will automatically appear on your new device.

- **Editing or Deleting a Contact:**

    1. Tap on the contact's name, then tap the "Edit" (pencil ✏️) icon. Make your changes and tap "Save," or scroll down to find the "Delete" option.

4.3 Sending Messages (SMS & MMS)

You can send text messages and photos to other phones.

- **How to Send a Text Message:**

    1. Open the **Messages** app (it looks like a colorful speech bubble 💬).

    2. Tap the "Compose" button (a pencil and paper icon or a "+" sign).

    3. In the "To" field, start typing the name of a contact, or type a phone number.

    4. Tap the text field that says "Enter message" and type your message using the keyboard.

5. Tap the **Send** button (it looks like a paper airplane ✈).

- **Sending a Photo or Video (MMS):**

    1. While composing a message, tap the **Attachment** icon (it looks like a paperclip 📎 or a plus "+" sign).

    2. Tap "Gallery" or "Camera."

    3. Select a photo from your gallery or take a new one.

    4. The photo will be added to your message. Just tap "Send" as usual.

- **Reading and Replying:**

    1. New messages will appear as a "notification" at the top of your

screen. You can tap it to open and reply directly.

2. All your conversations are saved as "threads" in the Messages app, so you can scroll up to see your history with any person.

4.4 Using Email
Your phone can handle all your email accounts.

- **Setting Up Your Email:**
    o Your phone likely has two apps: **Gmail** (for Gmail accounts) and **Samsung Email** (for all other accounts like Yahoo, Outlook, etc.).

- If you use Gmail, it's probably already set up from your Google Account.

- For other accounts (e.g., from your internet provider), open the **Samsung Email** app, tap "Add Account," and follow the steps. You'll need your email address and password.

- **Reading and Sending Email:**

  - **To read:** Tap on any email in your "Inbox."

  - **To compose a new email:** Tap the "Compose" (pencil ✏️) button.

    - **To:** Enter the recipient's email address.

- **Subject:** A brief description of the email.

- **Body:** Type your message in the large text area.

  o Tap the **Send** button (a paper airplane ✈).

4.5 Browsing the Internet with Samsung Internet

The Internet app is your gateway to the web.

- **Opening a Website:**

  1. Tap the **Internet** app.

  2. At the top, you'll see the "Address Bar." This is where you type website addresses (like www.news.com) or search terms (like "tomato soup recipe").

3. Type what you're looking for and tap "Go" on the keyboard.

- **Basic Navigation:**

    1. **Back (◀):** Goes to the previous page.

    2. **Forward (▶):** Goes to the next page (if you've gone back).

    3. **Tabs (☰ or ▢):** Shows all your open websites, like pages in a book. You can open multiple sites at once.

    4. **Bookmark (☆):** Saves a website to your favorites for easy access later.

Key Tips for Beginners & Seniors for Chapter 4:

- **Use the Speakerphone:** If you have a hard time hearing, the speakerphone function is your best friend during calls.

- **Talk to Text:** When typing a message or email, look for a **microphone** 🎤 icon on the keyboard. Tap it and just speak. Your phone will type the words for you. It's very accurate and saves time!

- **Emergency SOS:** You can set up a quick way to call for help. In **Settings > Safety and Emergency**, you can enable a feature to call emergency services by quickly pressing the Power button 5 times. It's good to have this set up, just in case.

- **You Can't Break It:** Feel free to explore the Phone and Messages apps. You can't break anything by tapping around. The "Back" gesture (swipe from the edge) is always there to get you out of a screen you didn't mean to open.

Chapter 5: Galaxy AI Features

This chapter introduces you to the "smart" or "AI" (Artificial Intelligence) features of your phone. Think of AI as a helpful assistant built into your device that can understand what you're doing and offer a hand. These features are designed to make your life easier, not more complicated.

5.1 Introduction to Galaxy AI

- **What is Galaxy AI?** It's a collection of tools on your phone that can perform intelligent tasks. These can range from translating a foreign menu in real-time to helping you write a perfectly worded text message.

- **Your AI Assistant:** You can interact with an AI assistant in two main ways:

- **Bixby:** Samsung's own voice assistant. Press and hold the **Power / Side Key** to talk to it and ask questions, set reminders, or control your phone with your voice.

- **Google Gemini:** A powerful AI from Google that can answer complex questions, help you write, and brainstorm ideas. You can often access it by saying "Hey Google" or through its app.

- **Key Idea:** You don't *have* to use these features, but they can be surprisingly helpful once you get the hang of them.

5.2 Circle to Search & Google Gemini Integration

This is one of the easiest and most impressive AI features to try.

- **What it Does:** Lets you search for anything on your screen without switching apps.

- **How to Use It:**

    1. You're looking at something—a photo, a text message, a webpage.

    2. **Press and hold the Home Button** (the spot at the very bottom of your screen where you swipe up to go home) **with one finger, OR press and hold with two fingers anywhere on the screen.** The screen will slightly dim.

3. Without lifting your finger, **circle, highlight, or tap** on the item you're curious about.

- See a beautiful plant in a photo? Circle it.
- Read an unfamiliar word in a news article? Highlight it.
- See a landmark in a friend's social media post? Tap on it.

4. A Google search result will pop up from the bottom of the screen, giving you information about what you selected.

- **A Simple Practice:** Go to a photo of a famous place, like the Eiffel Tower. Use

Circle to Search on it. You'll instantly get information about it. It's like having a search engine for the real world.

5.3 Live Translate & Interpreter

This turns your phone into a real-time translator, which is fantastic for travel or reading foreign languages.

- **Live Translate for Phone Calls:**
    - **What it Does:** Can translate a phone call between two languages in real time. You speak English, and the person on the other end hears it in Spanish, and vice-versa.

- **How to Use It:**

    1. Open the **Phone** app and go to **Settings > Call Assist > Live Translate**.

    2. Turn it on and choose your languages (e.g., English and Spanish).

    3. The next time you get a call from a number with that language, the translation will happen automatically.

- **Interpreter Mode:**

    - **What it Does:** Creates a split-screen translation for a face-to-face conversation. No phone call is needed.

- **How to Use It:**

    1. Add the "Interpreter" widget to your quick panel (swipe down from the top twice) for easy access.

    2. Tap it, select the languages, and talk. Your phone will display the translated text for both you and the other person to read.

5.4 AI Camera & Editing Tools (Your Digital Photo Lab)

Your phone's camera doesn't just take pictures; it helps you perfect them.

- **Generative Edit (Erase & Resize Objects):**

- **The "Magic Eraser":** Took a great photo but someone walked into the background? You can erase them.

    1. Open a photo in the **Gallery** app.
    2. Tap "Edit," then look for the **"Generative Edit"** or "Object Eraser" tool.
    3. Use your finger or the S Pen to color over the object or person you want to remove.
    4. Tap "Generate." The AI will analyze the area and fill it in seamlessly, as if the object was never there.

- **Recompose a Photo:** Want to make an object bigger or move it?
    1. In Generative Edit, you can often circle an object and then drag it to a new spot in the photo. The AI will intelligently reposition it.
- **Audio Eraser (For Videos):**
    - **What it Does:** If you recorded a video in a noisy place (like with loud wind or background chatter), this tool can isolate and reduce that unwanted noise, making the main subject's voice clearer.

- **How to Use It:**
    1. Open a video in the **Gallery** app and tap "Edit."
    2. Look for the "**Audio Eraser**" option (it might look like a sound wave).
    3. The phone will analyze the audio and show you sliders to reduce background noise.
- **Custom Filters:**
    - The AI can study your photo editing style and create a custom filter that applies the same look (e.g., brighter colors, warmer

tones) to all your photos with one tap.

5.5 Now Brief & Seamless Actions

This feature is like a personal secretary that learns your habits.

- **Now Brief:**
    - **What it Does:** Provides useful information on your lock screen or home screen without you asking. It might show you the weather, your next calendar appointment, your step count, or even remind you to leave for an appointment based on current traffic.
    - **How to Use It:** You don't need to do anything! It works

automatically. Just glance at your lock screen to see the "brief."

- **Seamless Actions:**
  - This is the AI working in the background to make things smooth. For example, if you copy an address from a text message and then open Google Maps, the phone might automatically suggest pasting that address for navigation. It connects your actions between apps.

Key Tips for Beginners & Seniors for Chapter 5:

- **Start with One Thing:** Don't feel pressured to learn all the AI features at once. Pick one that sounds interesting, like **Circle to Search**, and play with it for a day.

- **The "Undo" Button is Your Friend:** When editing photos with AI tools, there is always an "Undo" arrow. You can't permanently ruin a photo, so experiment without fear.

- **Internet Connection:** Many advanced AI features, like Generative Edit, require an internet connection to work because the processing is done on powerful servers, not just on your phone.

- **It's Okay to Ignore:** If a pop-up or suggestion from the AI feels annoying, you can usually swipe it away or turn off that specific notification in Settings.

The phone is there to help you, not the other way around.

Chapter 6: Camera Guide

Your Samsung Galaxy S26 Ultra has one of the most powerful camera systems on a phone. This chapter will help you understand how to use it to take fantastic photos and videos, moving from simple "point and shoot" to using its advanced features.

6.1 Camera Overview & Interface

Let's start by learning what you see on the screen when you open the Camera app.

- **How to Open the Camera Quickly:**
    - From any screen (even the lock screen), **double-press the Power / Side Key**. This is the fastest way to capture a moment.

- **Understanding the Camera Screen:**
  - **Viewfinder:** This is the main part of the screen, showing what the camera sees.
  - **Shutter Button:** The big circular button at the bottom. Tap it to take a photo. Press and hold to record a video.
  - **Mode Strip:** Near the bottom, you can swipe through different camera "modes" like PHOTO, VIDEO, PORTRAIT, and MORE.
  - **Top Icons:**
    - **Flash (⚡):** Turn the flash On, Off, or set to Auto.

- **Timer** (⏱): Sets a countdown (e.g., 3 or 10 seconds) before the photo is taken. Great for group photos where you need to jump in!
- **Settings** (⚙): Accesses the main camera settings menu.
- **Intelligent Scanning:** This helps the camera optimize for scenes, faces, and text. It's best to leave this on.
  - **Zoom Buttons:** You'll see numbers like 0.5, 1x, 2x, 5x, and 10x. Tapping these switches

between the different lenses on your phone.

- **0.5x (Ultra-Wide):** Captures a huge, sweeping view. Perfect for landscapes, architecture, and large groups.

- **1x (Main Wide):** The standard, all-purpose camera. Use this for most of your everyday photos.

- **3x, 5x, 10x (Telephoto):** These are for zooming in close to distant subjects, like wildlife or a performer on a stage. The

S26 Ultra's zoom is incredibly clear.

6.2 Core Photo & Video Modes

You don't need to be a pro. Start with these basic modes for great results.

- **PHOTO Mode (The Default):**
  - This is your "auto" or "point-and-shoot" mode. The camera automatically adjusts settings for the best possible photo.
  - **Just tap the shutter button.** The AI will recognize if you're taking a picture of a person, food, or a sunset and adjust colors and brightness accordingly.

- **PORTRAIT Mode:**
    - **What it Does:** Creates beautiful photos of people where the background is softly blurred (this effect is called "bokeh"), making the subject stand out.
    - **How to Use:** Switch to "PORTRAIT" mode, frame your subject, and take the picture. You can even adjust the blur level *after* the photo is taken in the Gallery app.
- **VIDEO Mode:**
    - Tap the VIDEO mode and press the shutter button to start recording. Press it again to stop.

- **For Stability:** Look for a "Steady" or "Super Steady" option in the video mode strip. Turn this on if you're walking while filming to make the video much smoother.

- **NIGHTOGRAPHY Mode:**

    - **What it Does:** Lets you take clear, bright photos in very dark environments without using the flash.

    - **How to Use:** Switch to "NIGHTOGRAPHY" mode. Hold the phone very still (rest it on a surface if you can). The phone will take a longer exposure, so it's important not to move until the photo is finished processing.

6.3 Advanced Features

Once you're comfortable, try these powerful tools.

- **PRO Mode:**
    - This gives you manual control, like a professional camera. **This is optional and for those who want to learn.**
    - You can adjust:
        - **ISO:** Controls the camera's sensitivity to light. Lower for bright days, higher for dark scenes.
        - **Shutter Speed:** Controls how long the shutter stays open. Fast to freeze action (like a splash), slow to

create light trails (like car headlights at night).

- **Don't be intimidated!** You can tap "AUTO" to let the phone handle it even in PRO mode.

• **200MP High Resolution:**

- In PHOTO mode, tap the "Ratio" icon at the top and select "200MP." This captures an incredibly detailed photo with a massive file size. It's best for landscapes in good lighting where you might want to print the photo very large or crop in deeply.

- **AI Zoom:**
    - When you zoom beyond 10x (up to 100x), the phone uses AI to keep the image as clear as possible. A small thumbnail window will appear to help you keep your subject in the frame, as it can be hard to hold steady at extreme zoom levels.

6.4 Tips for Taking Great Photos

- **Clean Your Lenses:** Gently wipe the camera lenses on the back with a soft, clean cloth. Smudges are the #1 cause of blurry, hazy photos.

- **Tap to Focus and Set Exposure:** Before taking a photo, tap on the screen on your main subject (like a person's face). This tells the camera what to focus on and also sets the brightness (exposure) correctly for that spot.

- **Hold Steady:** Try to hold the phone as still as possible when you press the shutter button, especially in lower light.

- **Use the Timer for Group Shots:** Set a 3 or 10-second timer, prop the phone up, and get in the picture with everyone else.

- **Experiment with Lenses:** Get in the habit of trying the 0.5x Ultra-Wide and the 5x Telephoto for the same scene. You might be surprised by the different and interesting photos you can get.

Key Tips for Beginners & Seniors for Chapter 6:

- **Stick with PHOTO Mode:** For your first few weeks, just use the standard PHOTO mode. It will do 95% of what you need perfectly.

- **The Zoom Buttons are Your Best Friend:** Instead of walking closer to something, try using the 2x or 5x zoom for a flattering portrait, or the 0.5x to get the entire building in the shot.

- **You Can't Waste Film:** The digital camera lets you take hundreds of photos. Take multiple shots of the same thing to ensure you get one you love. You can always delete the extras later.

- **Edit Your Photos:** Don't forget the AI editing tools from Chapter 5! If a photo is a little dark, you can open it in the Gallery, tap "Edit," and use the "Auto Adjust" button to often make it instantly better.

Chapter 7: Customization & Settings

This chapter is all about making your phone feel like *your* phone. You will learn how to change how it looks, how it sounds, and how it delivers information to you, creating an experience that is both comfortable and efficient.

7.1 Home Screen, Apps Screen, and Widgets

Think of your Home Screen as your desk—you can arrange everything just the way you like it.

- **The Basics:**
    - **Home Screen:** This is your main screen when you unlock the phone. It holds your favorite apps, widgets, and wallpaper.

- **Apps Screen:** This is your "filing cabinet" where all your apps are stored. To open it, swipe up from the bottom of the Home Screen.

- **Moving and Organizing Apps:**

  - **To Move an App:** Press and hold your finger on an app icon until the screen changes and you feel a vibration. Then, without lifting your finger, drag the app to a new spot on the Home Screen or even into the "dock" at the very bottom.

  - **To Create a Folder:** Drag one app icon on top of another. This creates a folder to group similar apps (e.g., "Games" or

"Banking"). You can tap the folder name to rename it.

- **To Remove an App:** Press and hold the app icon and drag it to the top of the screen where it says "Remove" or "Uninstall." **Don't worry:** "Remove" just takes it off the Home Screen; the app is still in your Apps Screen. "Uninstall" deletes the app from your phone completely.

- **Understanding Widgets:**

  - **What are Widgets?** They are "live" previews of app information that live on your Home Screen. They are like mini-apps that show you information without having to open the full app.

- **Examples:** A calendar widget showing your next event, a weather widget showing the current temperature, or a photo widget displaying a slideshow of your pictures.

- **How to Add a Widget:**

    1. Press and hold on an empty area of your Home Screen.

    2. Tap "**Widgets**" from the menu that appears.

    3. You'll see a list of all your apps that have widgets.

Find one you like (e.g., "Clock" or "Google Photos").

4. Press, hold, and drag the widget you want onto your Home Screen.

7.2 Themes, Wallpapers, and Always On Display (AOD)

Change the entire look and feel of your phone's display.

- **Changing Your Wallpaper:**
    - Your wallpaper is the background picture on your Home and Lock Screens.
    - **How to Change It:** Press and hold an empty area on the Home Screen > Tap "**Wallpaper and**

style" > You can choose from Samsung's gallery or tap "My photos" to use one of your own pictures. Tap "Set as wallpaper" when you're done.

- **Adjusting Text Size and Style:**

    o If the text is too small to read comfortably, you can make it bigger.

    o Go to **Settings** > **Display** > **Font size and style**. Use the slider to adjust the size until it's comfortable for you. You can also change the font style here.

- **Always On Display (AOD):**

    o **What it Does:** When your screen is locked and asleep, the AOD shows the time, date, battery level, and notifications in a dim, low-power format. You can just tap the screen to see this information without pressing any buttons.

- **How to Customize It:** Go to **Settings** > **Lock screen** > **Always On Display**. You can choose to have it always on, tap to show, or schedule it for certain times.

7.3 Sound and Vibration Settings
Make sure you can hear your phone ring and feel its alerts.

- **Adjusting Volume:**

- Use the **Volume Keys** on the side of the phone. A menu will appear on the screen. You can adjust the volume for:
    - **Media** (music, videos)
    - **Ringtone** (incoming calls)
    - **Notifications** (alerts for texts, emails)
    - **System** (other sounds)
- Tap the down arrow on the volume menu to see sliders for all of these.

- **Changing Your Ringtone:**
    - Go to **Settings** > **Sounds and vibration** > **Ringtone**.

- You can then tap on different sounds to hear a preview. Tap "OK" or "Apply" when you find one you like.

- **Turning on Vibration:**

    - It's a good idea to have both sound and vibration on, so you don't miss alerts.

    - Go to **Settings** > **Sounds and vibration**.

    - Toggle on "**Vibrate for calls**" and "**Vibration feedback**" (which gives a small buzz when you type or tap buttons).

7.4 Notifications and the Quick Panel

Managing the flood of information so it doesn't overwhelm you.

- **Understanding the Quick Panel:**
    - This is your control center. To open it, **swipe down from the very top of the screen.**
    - Here you'll find:
        - **Quick Settings Toggles:** Buttons for your most-used functions like Wi-Fi, Bluetooth, Flashlight, and Do Not Disturb. You can tap to turn them on or off.

- **Brightness Slider:** A big slider to quickly make your screen brighter or dimmer.
- **Notifications:** A list of all your recent alerts from apps.

- **Managing Notifications:**
    - **To View a Notification:** Just tap on it in the list to open the relevant app.
    - **To Dismiss a Single Notification:** Swipe it slightly to the left or right.
    - **To Control Which Apps Can Notify You:** Go to **Settings > Notifications > App notifications**. Here, you can

turn off notifications for apps that are too noisy (like games). This can make your phone much less distracting.

Key Tips for Beginners & Seniors for Chapter 7:

- **Start Simple:** Begin by just changing your wallpaper to a favorite photo of your family or a beautiful landscape. It's an instant personal touch.

- **Use Folders to Declutter:** If your Home Screen gets messy, create folders for "Social" (Facebook, Instagram), "Utilities" (Calculator, Flashlight), and "Games." It makes everything easier to find.

- **Make Text Larger:** Don't strain your eyes. Increasing the font size in the Display settings is one of the most important comfort adjustments you can make.

- **The Flashlight is in the Quick Panel:** Need a light? Swipe down from the top of your screen and tap the "Flashlight" icon. It's much faster than looking for an app!

- **You Can't Permanently Mess Anything Up:** Every change you make in this chapter can be undone. If you don't like a new wallpaper, just change it back. If your Home Screen is a mess, you can reset it to default in the settings. Experiment without fear.

Chapter 8: Productivity & Advanced Features

Your Galaxy S26 Ultra is more than just a phone; it's a powerful pocket computer. This chapter explores features that can help you be more productive, whether you're working from home, managing your health, or controlling your smart devices.

8.1 Samsung DeX: Your Phone as a PC

- **What it is:** A feature that lets you use your phone with a monitor, keyboard, and mouse to get a desktop computer-like experience. All your apps and files are right there.

- **How to Use It:**
  1. **Wired Connection (Simplest):** Connect your phone

to an external monitor or TV using a USB-C to HDMI adapter or cable.

2. **Wireless Connection:** Swipe down to open the Quick Panel and tap "Smart View." Select a compatible smart TV or wireless display, and then choose "Start now" under the DeX option.

- **What You'll See:** Your monitor will show a desktop with a taskbar, resizable app windows, and a file manager. You can use your phone as a touchpad or connect a Bluetooth keyboard and mouse.

- **Perfect For:** Writing long emails, working on spreadsheets, or browsing the web on a large screen without needing a traditional computer.

8.2 Multi-Window & Split-Screen for Multitasking

You can use two apps at the same time, side-by-side on your screen.

- **How to Activate Split-Screen:**

    1. Open the first app you want to use.
    2. Swipe up from the bottom and hold to see your recent apps.
    3. Tap the app's icon at the top of its window.
    4. Select "**Open in split screen view**."
    5. Your screen will split, and you'll be asked to select the second app.

- **Example Use Case:** You can have a web browser open on the top half of your screen to research a topic, and the Notes app open on the bottom half to jot down ideas.

- **Adjusting the Windows:** Drag the small divider bar between the two apps up or down to give one app more screen space.

8.3 Samsung Pass for Secure Logins

Tired of remembering dozens of passwords? Samsung Pass helps.

- **What it Does:** It uses your phone's secure biometrics (your fingerprint or face) to automatically log you into websites and apps on your device.

- **How to Set It Up:**

    1. Go to **Settings > Security and Privacy > Samsung Pass**.

    2. Follow the on-screen instructions to set it up with your Samsung account and biometrics.

- **How to Use It:** The next time you visit a website or app that requires a login, a prompt from Samsung Pass will appear. Simply verify with your fingerprint or face instead of typing your password.

8.4 Samsung Health & SmartThings Integration

Your phone is the hub for your well-being and smart home.

- **Samsung Health:**

  - **What it Does:** A built-in app to track your steps, monitor your sleep, record workouts, and even track your water intake.

  - **Getting Started:** Open the **Samsung Health** app. It will ask for basic information and then start counting your steps automatically. You can manually log workouts, weight, and more.

  - **Pro Tip:** For more accurate health data, consider pairing a Samsung Galaxy Watch, but the phone alone is a great start.

- **SmartThings:**
  - **What it Does:** A single app to control all your compatible smart home devices, like lights, plugs, thermostats, and TVs, from different brands.
  - **How to Set Up:**
    1. Open the **SmartThings** app.
    2. Tap the "+" sign to "Add Device."
    3. The app will automatically scan for devices on your Wi-Fi network. You can also add devices manually.

- **Creating a "Routine":** You can create automations. For example, a "Good Morning" routine could turn on your lights, adjust the thermostat, and read out your schedule when you say "Hey Google, good morning."

Key Tips for Beginners & Seniors for Chapter 8:

- **Start with Split-Screen:** Try using Split-Screen just once with two apps you use often, like Messages and your Calendar. It's a less intimidating way to experience multitasking.

- **Samsung Pass is a Lifesaver:** If you only ever use one advanced security feature, make it this one. It makes using the internet much easier and more secure.

- **DeX is a "Nice to Have":** Don't feel you need to use Samsung DeX. It's a powerful bonus feature for specific situations, not a requirement for everyday use.

- **SmartThings for Simple Control:** Even if you only have one or two smart lights, the SmartThings app is easier to use than juggling multiple different apps from different brands. It brings everything together.

- **Your Phone is a Step Counter:** Remember, the Samsung Health app is always working in the background. Check it at the end of the day to see how active you've been—it can be a great motivator!

This concludes the guided tour of the projected manual for the Samsung Galaxy S26 Ultra. You now have a comprehensive foundation for understanding and using its wide array of features, from the basic setup to advanced productivity tools. Remember, the best way to learn is to explore your device gently and without pressure. Enjoy your new phone

Printed in Dunstable, United Kingdom